*The Dollar, Debt,
and the Trade Deficit*

THE JOSEPH I. LUBIN MEMORIAL LECTURES

NUMBER 3

Anthony M. Solomon

Former Undersecretary of the Treasury
Former President and Chief Executive Officer
of the Federal Reserve Bank of New York

The Dollar, Debt, and the Trade Deficit

The Joseph I. Lubin Memorial Lectures
College of Business and Public Administration
New York University

NEW YORK UNIVERSITY PRESS
NEW YORK AND LONDON
1987

Library of Congress Cataloging-in-Publication Data

Solomon, Anthony M.
  The dollar, debt, and the trade deficit.

  (The Joseph I. Lubin memorial lectures; no. 3)
  1. Balance of trade—United States. 2. Debts,
External—United States. 3. Foreign exchange problem—
United States. 4. Export sales—United States.
I. Title. II. Series.
HF3031.S65 1987   382.1'7'0973   86-23651
ISBN 0-8147-7863-1

FOREWORD

This is the third volume in the Joseph I. Lubin Memorial Lectures series. It addresses the present and future value of the dollar, as well as the United States trade deficit and the nation's new international role as a net debtor.

Mr. Anthony Solomon is ideally suited to discuss these major issues. He is the recently retired president and chief executive officer of the Federal Reserve Bank of New York. Educated at the University of Chicago and Harvard University Mr. Solomon has served during his distinguished career in a number of significant posts within both the U.S. State Department and the U.S. Treasury. He has also taught at the Harvard Business School and served as a special consultant to President John F. Kennedy.

In this paper Mr. Solomon argues that the United States trade deficit has dangerous long-run consequences for the world. Specifically, continuing U.S. trade deficits of the magnitude experienced in recent years would, if unchecked, "leave the United States in the position of being an unacceptably large drain on the world's supply of savings and therefore a rogue elephant in the world's financial markets.'' The problem would best be solved, Mr. Solomon feels, if the United States were permitted ''to export its way out of the trade deficit,'' something which can best be accomplished by concerted international cooperation to lower the value of the dollar vis-à-vis the currencies of Japan and Europe. A failure of such cooperation, Mr. Solomon warns, is likely to lead to U.S. import restrictions which would be injurious to all concerned.

I am grateful to my assistants, Amanda Sherman and Virginia Moress, as well as to my secretary, Eileen Cassidy, for their help in handling the details of arranging this year's Lubin lecture. I am also grateful to the staff of the New York University Press for their efforts in producing this volume.

March 1, 1986   DANIEL E. DIAMOND
                                 Dean, College of
                                 Business and Public
                                 Administration

THE JOSEPH I. LUBIN
MEMORIAL LECTURES

The Joseph I. Lubin Memorial Lectures were established through the generosity of a distinguished trustee of New York University, the late Joseph I. Lubin. Mr. Lubin, who was a preeminent force in the business and philanthropic community, wished to provide a public forum for the discussion and practical application of economic and management theories.

This extraordinary humanitarian will also be remembered for his civic and philanthropic endeavors. He has enriched this city not only by New York University's Eisner & Lubin Auditorium, but also by his contributions of the Joseph I. Lubin Pace Schools of Business, the Joseph I. Lubin Syracuse House, and the Evelyn J. and Joseph I. Lubin Rehabilitation Center and Center for Learning Disabilities at the Albert Einstein College of Medicine. Mr. Lubin was a Gallatin Fellow and a Haskins Associate of the College of Business & Public Administration, New York University. He also served as a trustee of Syracuse and Pace Universities and of the Albert Einstein College of Medicine.

This volume is the third in the Joseph I. Lubin Memorial Lecture series and is modeled after our past distinguished Charles C. Moskowitz Memorial Lectures series. A complete listing of these lectures can be found on the following pages.

February, 1961   *Business Survival in the Sixties*
Thomas F. Patton, President and Chief Executive Officer
Republic Steel Corporation

November, 1961   *The Challenges Facing Management*
Don G. Mitchell, President
General Telephone and Electronics Corporation

November, 1962   *Competitive Private Enterprise Under Government Regulation*
Malcolm A. MacIntyre, President
Eastern Air Lines

November, 1963   *The Common Market: Friend or Competitor?*
Jesse W. Markham, Professor of Economics, Princeton University
Charles E. Fiero, Vice President, The Chase Manhattan Bank
Howard S. Piquet, Senior Specialist in International Economics, Legislative Reference Service, The Library of Congress

November, 1964   *The Forces Influencing the American Economy*
Jules Backman, Research Professor of Economics, New York University
Martin R. Gainsbrugh, Chief Economist and Vice President, National Industrial Conference Board

November, 1965   *The American Market of the Future*
Arno H. Johnson, Vice President and Senior Economist, J. Walter Thompson Company
Gilbert E. Jones, President, IBM World Trade Corporation
Darrell B. Lucas, Professor of Marketing and Chairman of the Department, New York University

November, 1966   *Government Wage-Price Guideposts in the American Economy*
George Meany, President, American Federation of Labor and Congress of Industrial Organizations
Roger M. Blough, Chairman of the Board and Chief Executive Officer, United States Steel Corporation
Neil H. Jacoby, Dean, Graduate School of Business Administration, University of California at Los Angeles

November, 1967   *The Defense Sector in the American Economy*
Jacob J. Javits, United States Senator, New York
Charles J. Hitch, President, University of California
Arthur F. Burns, Chairman, Federal Reserve Board

November, 1968   *The Urban Environment: How It Can Be Improved*
William E. Zisch, Vice-chairman of the Board, Aerojet-General Corporation
Paul H. Douglas, Chairman, National Commission on Urban Problems
Professor of Economics, New School for Social Research
Robert C. Weaver, President, Bernard M. Baruch College of the City University of New York
Former Secretary of Housing and Urban Development

November, 1969   *Inflation: The Problem It Creates and the Policies It Requires*
Arthur M. Okun, Senior Fellow, The Brookings Institution
Henry H. Fowler, General Partner, Goldman, Sachs & Co.
Milton Gilbert, Economic Adviser, Bank for International Settlements

March, 1971   *The Economics of Pollution*
Kenneth E. Boulding, Professor of Economics, University of Colorado
Elvis J. Stahr, President, National Audubon Society
Solomon Fabricant, Professor of Economics, New York University

Former Director, National Bureau of Economic Research

Martin R. Gainsbrugh, Adjunct Professor of Economics, New York University

Chief Economist, National Industrial Conference Board

April, 1971

Young America in the NOW World

Hubert H. Humphrey, Senator from Minnesota

Former Vice President of the United States

April, 1972

Optimum Social Welfare and Productivity: A Comparative View

Jan Tinbergen, Professor of Development Planning, Netherlands School of Economics, Nobel Laureate

Abram Bergson, George E. Baker Professor of Economics, Harvard University

Fritz Machlup, Professor of Economics, New York University

April, 1973

Fiscal Responsibility: Tax Increases or Spending Cuts?

Paul McCracken, Edmund Ezra Day University, Professor of Business Administration, University of Michigan

Murray L. Weidenbaum, Edward Mallinckrodt Distinguished University Professor, Washington University

Lawrence S. Ritter, Professor of Finance, New York University

Robert A. Kavesh, Professor of Finance, New York University

March, 1974   *Wall Street in Transition: The Emerging System and its Impact on the Economy*

Henry G. Manne, Distinguished Professor of Law, Director of the Center for Studies in Law and Economics, University of Miami Law School

Ezra Solomon, Dean Witter Professor of Finance, Stanford University

March, 1975   *Leaders and Followers in an Age of Ambiguity*

George P. Schultz, Professor, Graduate School of Business, Stanford University President, Bechtel Corporation

March, 1976   *The Economic System in an Age of Discontinuity: Long-Range Planning or Market Reliance?*

Wassily Leontief, Nobel Laureate, Professor of Economics, New York University

Herbert Stein, A. Willis Robertson Professor of Economics, University of Virginia

March, 1977   *Demographic Dynamics in America*
                     Wilber J. Cohen, Dean of the School of Ed-
                         ucation and Professor of Education and of
                         Public Welfare Administration, Univer-
                         sity of Michigan
                     Charles F. Westhoff, Director of the Office
                         of Population Research and Maurice Dur-
                         ing Professor of Demographic Studies,
                         Princeton University

March, 1978   *The Rediscovery of the Business Cycle*
                     Paul A. Volcker, President and Chief Exec-
                         utive Officer, Federal Reserve Bank of
                         New York

March, 1979   *Economic Pressure and the Future of the Arts*
                     William Schuman, Composer
                     Roger L. Stevens, Chairman of the Board of
                         Trustees, John F. Kennedy Center for the
                         Performing Arts

April, 1980   *Presidential Promises and Performance*
                     McGeorge Bundy, Professor of History, Fac-
                         ulty of Arts and Science, New York
                         University
                     Edmund S. Muskie, Former U.S. Senator
                         from Maine, Secretary of State

| March, 1981 | *Econometric Models as Guides for Decision-Making* |
| | *Lawrence R. Klein,* Benjamin Franklin Professor of Finance and Economics, University of Pennsylvania, Nobel Laureate |

| March, 1982 | *The American Economy, 1960–2000* |
| | *Richard M. Cyert,* President, Carnegie-Mellon University |

December, 1983	*Reaganomics: Meaning, Means, and Ends*
	John Kenneth Galbraith, Paul M. Warburg Professor of Economics Emeritus, Harvard University
	Paul W. McCracken, Edmund Ezra Day Distinguished University Professor of Business Administration, The University of Michigan, and Chairman, Council of Economic Advisers. American Institute for Public Policy Research

Note: All but the last seven volumes of The Charles C. Moskowitz Memorial Lectures were published by New York University Press. The 1977, 1978, 1979, 1980, 1981, 1982, and 1983 lectures were published by The Free Press.

THE JOSEPH I. LUBIN
MEMORIAL LECTURES

March, 1984   *The World Banking System: Outlook in a Context of Crisis*
Andrew F. Brimmer, President of Brimmer & Company Inc. and Chairman of the Monetary Policy Forum

December, 1984   *The Deficits: How Big? How Long? How Dangerous?*
Daniel Bell, Henry Ford II Professor of Social Sciences, Harvard University
Lester Thurow, Gordon Y. Billard Professor of Economics and Management, Massachusetts Institute of Technology

December, 1985   *The Dollar, Debt, and the Trade Deficit*
Anthony M. Solomon, Former Undersecretary of the Treasury, Former President and Chief Executive Officer of the Federal Reserve Bank of New York

CONTENTS

THE DOLLAR, DEBT,
AND THE TRADE DEFICIT

As we pass beyond the halfway point of this decade, it is natural to take stock of how far we have come in managing world economic and financial problems as well as our own national problems. Viewed in terms of that relatively short span of time, the changes have been striking, both in the content of the difficulties that face the world and in the contours of the debate over causes, remedies, and policy priorities. In several respects, what were thought to be highly complex, unsolvable problems have turned out to be less intractable than we feared. But in the process, a new array of problems has emerged. They are every bit as serious as the original ones, and at least as difficult to come to grips with.

• Whereas five years ago it seemed that it would take a generation of painful adjustment to weaken the grip of the Organization of Petroleum Exporting Countries (OPEC) over world oil prices, we now have generally soft oil markets and some concern about the potential for a permanent glut of excess supply.

• Whereas five years ago the general expectation was that the dollar would remain more or less permanently weak in the exchange markets, always vulnerable to further diversification by both public and private holders of dollar assets, the problem has now become the prolonged overvaluation of the dollar in terms of trade. The high dollar has crippled large parts of the U.S. manufacturing industry and left this country with a trade deficit the likes of which no one could have predicted a half decade ago.

• Whereas at the beginning of the 1980s the world's banks scrambled to lend ever larger amounts throughout the developing world, the subsequent debt crisis has left banks with large exposures which many of them wish they had never built up. The debt problem of many less developed countries (LDCs) appears to have permanently changed the makeup and the behavior of global financial markets and greatly reduced the number of regular market participants. At the same time, it has put immense strains on the resources and ingenuity of the International Monetary Fund (IMF), the World Bank, and other multilateral institutions.

• Whereas five years ago the threat of ever escalating inflation preoccupied economic policy-making and the attitudes of the general public, whereas five years ago farm land in the Midwest was doubling in price every six months, whereas precious metals were seen as providing limitless (and, to some purportedly sophisticated investors, riskless) opportunity, we now have seen the end of the inflationary spiral, the virtual collapse of inflationary expectations in most of the world's commodity markets, widespread financial distress, and a nagging concern over a secular trend to disinflation.

• Whereas five years ago an American administration was effectively criticized for the irresponsibility of incurring a $40 billion budget deficit, the public has lately been numbed by argument over deficits exceeding $200 billion, but totally baffled by the fact that while all segments of the political spectrum decry the deficits nothing seems to be done.

• Finally, whereas half a decade ago, Milton Friedman was the latest winner of the Nobel Prize in Economics for teaching the overriding importance of the money supply, this year a dyed-in-the-wool Keynesian and frequent debate adversary of Friedman's, MIT's Franco Modigliani, has been picked for that prestigious award. It must leave an outsider bewildered as to what brand of economic thought, if any, is genuinely true, believable and capable of predicting the impact of future economic policies.

I can assure you that even those of us who have spent an extensive part of our careers in economic policy jobs and who have taken part in the debates of recent years are not much better off in sorting out the conflicting judgments of competing economic theories. Economic analysis, however careful and objective, is inherently imperfect, and its conclusions are imprecise. We simply don't know how certain anyone can be in interpreting economic conditions, or in diagnosing what precisely has gone wrong and why; or, in prescribing remedies that are likely to be effective and at the same time are capable of being implemented through the political process.

What I suppose we do know for sure is that the financial markets, the business community and the public are confronted with rapid change in the economy and hear constantly of a seemingly endless litany of economic problems. But they have no handy tool or device for getting a sound perspective. They seek a structure, a way of ordering their thinking and reaching their own judgments about which problems are worth worrying about and which are not. Instead, in the kind of world we live in, every conceivable problem in the economic area attracts attention from the media. There's no end to experts, economists, or financial market people willing to give an opinion on one side of an issue or another. Consequently, most of the time the public is overloaded by a barrage of news commentary and rhetoric. Yet the public is left with a sense of incompleteness and with an unsatisfied appetite to get past the headlines to the true significance of the problem.

I think that it's particularly worthwhile to keep in the back of our minds this key distinction between what are fundamental problems and what are subordinate or derivative problems when we assess the international dimensions of the U.S. economic condition. The main statistics characterizing that condition are reasonably well known:

• Our trade deficit this year will exceed $140 billion, and the more inclusive current account measure (which folds in both trade in services and net investment income) will be nearly as large.

• The dollar, even after declining by some 10 percent on average from its peaks of late winter, is still about 25 percent higher than in 1980–82, when the current account was last in approximate balance.

• Private capital inflows to the United States, the logical counterpart of a current account deficit, will exceed $130 billion this year. They reflect heavy foreign investments in our securities markets, some net direct investment inflow, continued sizable movements of short-term funds from the Eurodollar market into our domestic banking system, and the familiar large errors and omissions component.

• Large trade and current account surpluses by Japan, perhaps reaching $40 billion this year, have made Japan the focus for vocal criticism for allowing unfair trading practices to continue. But the trade practices issue is not confined to Japan. Many other Asian and European countries also have moved into substantial surplus and also have less than free access to their domestic markets.

These massive trade imbalances and currency misalignments are dangerous. Eventually they must be eliminated. But until the agreement of the Group of Five (G-5) finance ministers was reached in September 1985, there was no obvious mechanism in operation that would tend to promote the needed adjustments.

That agreement represented a profound turnaround in attitude by the U.S. government. In a real sense, it signified a return to sanity. In my judgment, Secretary of the Treasury, James Baker deserves to be commended for grasping the urgency of the problem and getting behind an important initiative. Any further delay might have done irreparable harm to the world trading system.

However, as useful as the agreement has been so far, it is by no means certain to achieve the degree of positive results that will calm protectionist emotions in the U.S. Congress and keep things from degenerating into a nasty and not readily reversible slide into competitive trade restrictions. Sober heads have prevailed for the moment, but the frustrations and bitterness that arose out of an atmosphere of indifference and unconcern about the costs of large-scale trade imbalances have not disappeared; they are only submerged. Consequently, a fuller appreciation of the causes of the current condition is absolutely indispensable because there is often less than a sound understanding of what is fundamental in this whole area.

Let me expand on these general remarks by organizing the discussion under three headings:

• First, the external position of the U.S.—is it alarming that the U.S. has become a net debtor country?

• Second, the trade deficit—is it a fairness issue, or one of economics?

• Third, the dollar—why did it get so high and what further treatment is appropriate?

The U.S. as a Net Debtor Country

During 1985 the United States has become a net debtor country. The foreign assets owned by U.S. residents are now smaller than the U.S. assets owned by foreigners. That milestone, which represents a sharp reversal of the situation of just a few years ago when the U.S. net asset position exceeded $140 billion, has attracted a great deal of commentary, not all of which has been very instructive. To some, the term net debtor nation sounds somewhat menacing. It conjures up images of a Mexico or Brazil and the specter of default, insolvency, or worse. To others, it simply sounds unseemly; they ask how a nation as rich and powerful as the United States could be indebted to the rest of the world. To still others, being a net debtor nation implies a vague loss of sovereignty, as if the creditors of the United States government could somehow dictate terms to the world's largest debtor.

These particular fears are certainly exaggerated but they are not altogether unfounded. To be sure, on a strictly analytical basis, being a net debtor nation in and of itself does not have profound significance. It does mean that the nation will receive less in investment income than it will pay and those net remittances abroad will add to our already massive current account deficit. As a matter of arithmetic, the larger the net debtor position, the larger the current account deficit. Put another way, the larger the net debtor position, the greater the improvement in the merchandise trade deficit will have to be to achieve any particular reduction in our current account deficit. Indeed, if ultimately we should wish to reduce the current account deficit all the way to zero (a daunting and virtually impossible task for the next five years), it will mean the U.S. will have to swing all the way to a sizable trade surplus and continue to run a trade surplus indefinitely. Of course, there are other less ambitious goals that would require less of a turnaround in the trade position. But the point is simply this: The United States has been accustomed to earning net income from the rest of the world and that has changed—maybe permanently, but at least for the rest of this century.

While in coldly analytical terms being a net debtor nation even for the United States need not be a source of alarm, moving into that status does symbolize the awesome dimension of our international imbalance. Thus, it can easily have an important psychological effect on the financial markets and the willingness of foreign investors to accumulate ever increasing amounts of dollar assets. Concern will obviously grow in direct proportion to the size of the net debt. If over the next four years the United States continues to run current account deficits of the magnitude that it has had this year, the net debt of the United States will increase to over half a trillion dollars. Over that four-year period we will have to improve our trade position by something on the order of $50 billion from its present level just to pay the interest on the debt accumulated during that time. The longer the trend continues, the greater the adjustment burden on the trade side, all with a continuing vulnerability to the psychology of the foreign investor who must remain highly confident in our prospects. Is that likely?

Some people would argue that there's nothing to worry about as long as we maintain sound economic policies, fiscal and monetary. If we maintain reasonably adequate economic growth and keep inflation low, they say, we will continue to offer attractive outlets to foreign savers, outlets they will not be able to obtain anywhere else in the world as safely and with as good a yield as in the United States.

That argument is fine as far as it goes. But it neglects two important considerations: (1) It's very likely that foreigners will increasingly question the wisdom of our economic policy stance unless we have a major change in fiscal policy. The more indebted this country becomes to the rest of the world, the more visible and worrisome the large U.S. federal government deficit will appear and the greater the overall threat it would pose to foreign confidence.

(2) Moreover, to achieve a substantial improvement in the trade deficit year in and year out is almost certainly going to take a sustained downward correction in the value of the dollar. But as foreign investors become more and more aware of the need for the U.S. trade account to improve, they will also become more aware of the inevitability of the substantial correction in the value of the dollar. That sense that the dollar will come down is in itself a deterrent to continuing capital inflows.

In a nutshell, the true problem the United States faces in becoming a substantial net debtor country is that the situation sets up a logical conundrum: For it to be self-sustaining, foreigners must be constantly wrong about the course of exchange rates. They must continually judge U.S. dollar investments to be attractive as to both yield and safety. Almost certainly, that entails a sense that the dollar will rise or at least stay reasonably strong. Yet, at the same time, the dollar has to fall enough to create sufficient improvement in the trade account to keep the current account deficit constant.

To put the same point in terms familiar to dealers in the foreign exchange markets, the more logical scenario is that the kind of bullish psychology toward the United States that is needed to finance the current account deficit would also be likely to foster a strong dollar. But that would imply an accompanying rise in the current account deficit—just the opposite of the needed economic adjustment. Over time, the growing current account deficits would force the U.S. into the position of being a greater and greater drain on the world's financial resources.

Few economists have asked their computer

models what might have happened if the dollar's exchange rate had remained around levels reached before the G-5 initiative in September. Their estimates suggested that the U.S. might have been absorbing nearly half of the annual net new savings of the rest of the world by 1990. While possible as an intellectual exercise, one has to wonder whether that result would not be way beyond the capacity of foreign nations to permit.

To sum up, becoming a net debtor country is not in itself a fundamental problem. There have been countries, for example Japan in the 1960s and 1970s, which were net debtor countries for extended periods of time without serious adverse economic impact. Just the fact of being a net debtor country is not necessarily poisonous to the atmosphere in the exchange markets. But for the United States, fundamentally at stake is the ability to sustain increasingly large current account deficits in the second half of the 1980s. Without any obvious source of adjustment, sustained current account deficits would ultimately leave the United States in the position of being an unacceptably large drain on the world's supply of savings and therefore a kind of rogue elephant in the world's financial markets.

Trade Deficits: Unfairness or Economics?

Let me now turn to my second heading for assessing the international dimensions of the U.S. economic condition. I've been arguing that the true problem is the size and trend of the U.S. current account, heavily dominated by the growing merchandise trade imbalance and worsened by an adverse swing in net investment income. That is a real problem, reflecting important differences in broad economic trends between the United States and other major countries.

The way the headlines play this story, however, is to equate the trade deficit problem with a trade unfairness problem or a trade barrier problem. Admittedly it's true that other countries are not as receptive to foreign products, not just American products, as they might be. Most businessmen feel that the U.S. market is the most open and that proposition can be readily confirmed by talking to businessmen in Hong Kong, Malaysia, Brazil or any number of other countries. The U.S. market is not perfectly open, but it is certainly much more accessible than most other countries in most merchandise categories. Japan is usually cited as unreceptive to imports, but business executives, whether in the U.S. or in the LDCs, also cite Italy and France, and on some products even Britain, as having markets that are far less than open. Moreover, many LDCs have maintained for some years import-substitution policies that explicitly discriminate against foreign products, and of course several of them have closed their markets even further because of the scarcity of foreign exchange, which is due to the debt crisis.

Together, those various trade barriers have an impact on the composition of trade balances—on the precise character of the exports we can sell and the precise character of the imports that compete here in our market. Yet, the barriers themselves do not explain a very great portion of the actual magnitude of the large and growing trade imbalance.

What is the true source of the U.S. trade deficit? The answer has to be found in the area of macroeconomics—in the operation and interaction of the economies at large and in the net surpluses and deficits for each sector of the economy.

Put another way, a large current account deficit for the United States reveals a very severe savings deficit. It shows that we spend more than we produce. We rely heavily on the rest of the world to provide the savings that we're not generating ourselves. On the other side of the coin is the case of the Japanese. To a greater extent than any other country, Japan provides savings to the rest of the world by means of a growing current account surplus largely made up of a huge trade surplus. The Japanese savings are going to the rest of the world because Japanese investors have judged opportunities outside Japan—certainly in the short run and probably also in the long run—to be more lucrative than potential investment opportunities at home. That savings are exported and a current account surplus is run exposes a relative lack of investment opportunities. For the time being, there is a symbiotic relationship between the net saver, the Japanese most notably, and the net user of funds, the United States and some other countries with deficits.

The United States' savings insufficiency problem arises largely—but not solely—because of the U.S. federal government budget deficit. It's running at a $200 billion-a-year rate. It cannot be expected to diminish significantly without major compromises between the Congress and the Administration. That deficit represents dissaving. It overburdens the already limited savings of the U.S. private sector which itself is doing considerable investing in plant, equipment, houses, and consumer durables like cars, which requires financing. Because of the large federal government deficit, the U.S. starts off with a savings shortfall that overwhelms the savings-generating potential of the rest of the economy and makes it impossible for domestic credit demands to be met in full from domestic sources.

There are other countries, Japan for example, which also have large government deficits. Yet they generate very large net savings at the national level because the private sector in Japan has a very substantial surplus. That's not the case for the United States, partly because of a relative lack of savings incentives similar to those found in Japan, partly because of tax incentives to borrow that generate large-scale purchases of housing and other consumer durables and partly because of habit, culture, customs, and many other things that will take a very long time to change—and may never change.

But the fact remains that a substantial part of the savings shortfall relative to domestic credit demands does reflect the impact of policy, both purposeful and inadvertent, and that shortfall has to take the form of a trade and current account deficit.

The device that sets up the market incentives to create that correspondence between a net savings shortfall and a current account deficit is the exchange rate of the dollar. Even as our domestic savings imbalance grew, the high dollar multiplied the incentives to buy abroad, undermined incentives to buy U.S. products, and, therefore, left us with a growing trade and current account deficit just equal to our savings shortfall.

From the point of view, however, of individual industries that have been hit by foreign competition, the reaction has naturally been that the trading system itself is unfair, that the United States market is disproportionately open, and that they deserve protection.

Could that trade problem have been solved simply by removing the barriers that other countries have to foreign products? It may seem counterintuitive but the clear answer is no. For one thing the magnitude of distortions in world trade produced by those barriers is relatively moderate in scale. Even if they were removed overnight, they would not generate major trade flows into those countries. Even more important, they would generate trade flows into those countries from countries throughout the world, not only from the United States. In fact, in the presence of a large U.S. savings shortfall and the superstrong dollar, it is very unlikely that American products would be able to take advantage of freer markets.

Take the example of Japan and beef. At dollar exchange rates reached in 1985, if Japan had completely lifted its controls on imports of foreign beef, would the U.S. beef producers have sold more in Japan? Very unlikely. More likely would have been a substantial increase in beef exports from Argentina, Australia, and other beef-producing countries. The incentives to buy American beef would have been very much less impressive than some people might think.

So, trade barriers are headline-making concerns. They are legitimate sources of complaint by companies here and abroad that are affected by them, but they don't reach the root of the problem: insufficient savings, perpetuated by massive budget deficits, and adverse incentives for buying U.S. goods, perpetuated by an overvalued dollar.

The Dollar: Causes and Cures

Let us then turn to the problem of the dollar which used to be given far too little attention but has lately gotten considerable exposure both in the headlines and in debates among academic economists, market people, and government officials. What, if anything, should be done about the dollar's value in respect to other currencies? How can it be done? Is it worth doing?

There will always be tension when talking about the value of the dollar internationally because at least initially the main impact is redistributional. Some people gain and some people lose. I have noticed that technically oriented economists have some trepidation in getting involved with the issue at all, because judgments about the value of the dollar are essentially judgments about who should get those benefits and who should absorb costs. The main beneficiaries of a strong dollar are fairly obvious—they are a number of foreign producers and all domestic consumers. The main losers are some domestic producers and their workers. The relative benefit or cost depends on the actual responsiveness of markets to changes in exchange rates and the speed by which fluctuations show up in market prices of goods.

For example, anybody who looked at the price of a Mercedes-Benz, especially when the dollar was at its peak in March 1985, realized that at the very same time similar models were selling in Germany for a dollar equivalent that was half as big as the amount of dollars that car was selling for in New York. That shows that the international markets in goods are not perfect. The full impact of exchange rate changes does not pass through to the consumer of imported products. In this particular example, the clear beneficiary is the German auto company, which preferred higher profit margins to increasing even further its market share in volume terms.

In other products, however, the flow through to the consumer is relatively rapid. That is more frequently the case when the currency is falling. For example, in the last three years the strong dollar from the perspective of the European consumer was a problem because it imposed higher costs for basic commodities priced in dollars, like oil. The impact of the strong dollar was more than enough to wipe out any benefits to Europe from weakening oil prices. Evaluating the problem of the dollar depends on where you sit, and what you buy, and to whom you sell.

By now there is a widespread realization that a major portion of the deterioration in the U.S. trade account has been directly and indirectly caused by the strong dollar. Whether that share is 50 percent or 75 percent is of secondary importance. The high dollar penalizes U.S. exporters in foreign markets, and particularly in third-world markets where the U.S. has to compete head-on against Japanese and European competitors. It has also been a strong inducement for foreigners to expand market share for products that they have capacity to produce for the

U.S. market. In the process, U.S. imports have surged.

While the strong dollar lies at the root of the trade problem, there is an accompanying benefit. The strong dollar has been associated with large-scale capital flows into this country. In the absence of those capital inflows, U.S. interest rates would have to have been substantially higher to balance the supply and demand for credit. Instead, through the current account deficit, the U.S. has imported savings, augmenting its own pool of savings, which was insufficient relative to domestic credit demands. That augmented pool of savings has been enough to produce interest rates in our credit markets that are lower than if we had generated those savings ourselves. Just how much lower is a matter of conjecture, and one needs to look at the available econometric estimates, simplistic as they are, with great caution. But these estimates suggest the impact is quite significant, on the order of two or three percentage points, rather than one-quarter or one-half percent.

Thus, there has been a clear line of causation from heavy domestic credit demands to a strong dollar and to a large current account deficit. It is also obvious that the principal source for much of those heavy credit demands is the huge deficit being run by the federal government. So the strong dollar and the large government deficit have somehow been connected—at least in the case of the United States.

This does not mean that *all* countries which mismanage their fiscal policy and end up with large government deficits also end up with strong currencies. The more typical example is just the opposite. Large deficits are typically associated with downward pressure on the currency, not with strength. Here there are many examples: The pound or the Italian lira during the period 1975–1976 are as good illustrations as any. Sometimes governments have big budget deficits but are able to offset some downward pressure on their currencies by applying fairly rigorous exchange controls, or by orchestrating large-scale foreign currency borrowing in international capital markets, inducing, somewhat artificially, a countervailing inflow of funds. But eventually reality catches up. Any potential investor is certainly aware of the danger of authorities' seeking to finance the local currency budget by inflating the money supply. That carries grave risks both for inflation and for the exchange rate. Put in historical context, it is implausible that, by themselves, large U.S. government budget deficits made the dollar strong or would keep it strong indefinitely.

What distinguishes this country from others is that foreign investors have counted on American monetary authorities not to finance government deficits by overinflating the money supply. Monetary policy makers were prepared to see higher real interest rates materialize in the financial market as part of an overall strategy of keeping inflation low. That, in fact, happened. A general belief among foreign investors has been that the Federal Reserve would not monetize the budget deficits but would aim to keep inflation low, and would react to any temporary periods of excessive money growth by tightening up before inflationary expectations worsened.

Common sense would suggest that an initiative to lower the budget deficit would make investors more confident in the long-term ability of the Federal Reserve to maintain an inflation-containment policy. With less of a budget deficit to worry about, the Federal Reserve would be able to pursue its monetary objectives in a more tranquil environment. Certainly that kind of prospect would be a natural attraction to foreign investors and could precipitate substantial dollar buying in the exchange markets. In sum, it's certainly true that dollar interest rates have been high enough to attract considerable foreign investment. But it is not necessarily true that eliminating the budget deficit would be regarded as an occasion to reduce those flows, at least all at once.

This particular line of reasoning is worth considering, but it should not be taken to imply that budget deficits are harmless. They are not. They cause imbalances, such as the trade deficit, which eventually pose grave long-term risks and which must eventually be reduced. But when we seriously evaluate the full range of factors that have caused the dollar to be so strong in recent years, we find that a lot of the motivations reflect broader perceptions about the relative attractiveness of investing in the United States as opposed to other countries and that those choices were not mainly motivated by purely economic or relative yield considerations. In fact, during this entire period, the U.S. budget deficit has lurked in the background as a negative factor for the dollar. It served as a source of potential distrust. But throughout all this time the United States has been given the benefit of the doubt by foreign investors. These investors guess that inevitably the Congress and the administration will come to a meaningful compromise that deals with the budget deficit because it was in our national interest to do so. To me, it is instructive that the dollar's decline from its peak levels of early 1985 coincided with an erosion of some of that faith in our ability to get the budget deficit under control.

What are some of these factors that have generated investment in the dollar that are distinguishable from straight real yield considerations? To begin with, many foreign investors frequently cite the size and ease of access to our financial markets as the prime ingredient for attracting institutional funds, particularly from Japanese institutions. Undoubtedly the great depth and sophistication of our securities markets must matter. But it's worth remembering that those attractions were not sufficient to keep the dollar from falling sharply in the late 1970s. Confidence then was very different.

A further part of the flow has simply been flight capital seeking access to our markets, particularly because our capital markets are anonymous. Foreign investors could deal in them in substantial magnitude without being detected, especially by their own tax authorities. That gave a tremendous advantage to the dollar when a number of countries got into serious economic difficulties in recent years.

Apart from the special circumstances surrounding the flow of flight capital from the LDCs, a substantial volume of funds has been drawn to the dollar from Europe, primarily because of a set of factors that are as much psychological as economic.

At the heart of the matter are concerns about perceived structural weaknesses in Europe and the apparent lack of any credible program to treat those problems. Thus, continued slow, inadequate growth

in Europe has been a key stimulus for flow of funds
into the dollar. To a number of European investors
of diverse backgrounds, the primary motivation for
acquiring assets in the United States has been defen-
sive, a reaction to what they have viewed as limited
potential at home, rather than a clear preference for
U.S. policies.

Perhaps equally important, foreign investors have
sifted through various and sometimes conflicting
statements from the Reagan Administration that suggested that the President was in favor of a strong
dollar, viewing it as a positive verdict on his economic program. Apart from the details of policy,
foreign investors are highly sensitive to what they
believe to be the official attitude towards the dollar,
and for a long time the sense that a strong dollar was
sought by the President heavily colored the investment decisions of market participants.

Thus, while capital flows have been partially re-
sponsive to changes in relative yields, those changes
have not been the sole deciding influence, particularly in periods where exchange markets have taken
on more of a speculative character.

However, until September 1985, in Washington,
the main strand of economic advice was against using
policy levers, especially foreign-exchange-market
intervention, to influence capital flows and the value
of the dollar. Some were against it on ideological
grounds. They simply did not approve of interfer-
ence in the market. But there were other economists
without that ideological leaning who reached the
same conclusion on analytical grounds. They gave
less weight to noneconomic, long-term, political, or
psychological factors that have a major influence on

the direction and magnitude of capital flows. Instead they focused more narrowly on economic factors, almost to the total exclusion of these other factors. With some justification they argued that the causality ran from budget deficits to high real interest rates to the strong dollar. While this analysis is not wrong, it is incomplete—and from a policy perspective it had the unfortunate side effect of breeding inertia and building a reluctance to do anything about the strong dollar. A genuine feeling prevailed that nothing could be done until the budget deficit was first reduced. And, of course, that reduction has not been forthcoming.

My own view is that an excessively pessimistic view of the potential effectiveness of other levers, particularly of concerted central bank intervention, allowed the dollar's overvaluation to get out of hand, do great economic damage, and incite protectionist demands. It is a judgment based primarily on practical experience. I have seen well-planned intervention operations work, although I concede that intervention in the exchange markets is not always fully successful. Effectiveness usually depends on accompanying monetary and fiscal actions, or the credible promise of action, to change market psychology. But even if there are no changes in the shape and the thrust of overall economic policies, intervention can have a useful effect in dealing with speculative movements in markets. We saw an illustration of that in February and early March 1985 when the markets went on a very fast bandwagon and a moderate amount of well-timed intervention by European central banks played a constructive role in bringing a halt to that speculative bubble. And

I believe we saw another constructive illustration in recent weeks.

My sense is that a real shift toward pragmatism is embodied in the policy change that the Administration announced back in September 1985. The Group of Five countries agreed on a new approach that recognized that the dollar's value had gotten far out of line. That policy shift got some immediate results, certainly without any instant change in the U.S. budget deficit, policy toward which continues to be up in the air. That shift in policy could have happened sooner if the belief that budget deficits necessarily entailed a high dollar—and that nothing but reducing the deficit could be done about the value of the dollar—had not been so widely held among some otherwise distinguished economists. Less dogmatic policy views also would have been salutary. The U.S. role in the G-5 decision signals that more pragmatic approach and, in turn, colors the psychological view of market participants—in my view, in the proper direction.

To be sure, there are some risks in embarking on the new program. A decline in the dollar is bound to have some negative effect on U.S. inflation. And, therefore, care must be taken to avoid what some have referred to as a "crash landing." As long as the current account deficit remains, large capital inflows are needed to offset it. Thus, the more skillfully the dollar's decline is managed, the less threat there will be to the sustainability of that needed flow. And, therefore, the less upward pressure there will need to be on U.S. interest rates. But even despite these risks, the overall shift in approach is certain to lead in the direction we need to go.

Conclusion

My purpose today has been to try to shed some light on how we should distinguish between what are primarily surface phenomena and what are the fundamental economic problems from which those secondary problems are derived. I do not claim that concern over the United States' becoming a net debtor country or concern over the degree of openness of foreign markets is unwarranted. Put in the proper perspective they are legitimate aspects of the overall situation that needs to be corrected. But I do maintain that these are subordinate problems that stem from a more basic disequilibrium—a misordering of U.S. taxing and spending priorities, and a failure of other industrial countries to reinvigorate their economies and deal with their own structural weaknesses and domestic imbalances.

These fundamentals must be addressed and there is reason to believe that the G-5 agreement of September 1985 represents a promising start in terms of facing up to the difficult choices required. But even under the best of circumstances, time will be needed to construct the appropriate long-term program and to get it implemented and to prove to the markets that positive results are being achieved. In the interim, it is disheartening to read press reports of statements by a few important Europeans—notably Karl Otto Poehl, the president of Germany's central bank—that leave the impression that they are not fully behind the objectives of the policy initiative. They ought to ask themselves how a meaningful reduction in the U.S. current account deficit can be made without a change in market incentives, which requires a substantial change in exchange rates. They ought to ask themselves, too, where U.S. exporting can be expanded if not to countries with strong trade positions and external debt constraints. That means to Japan and Europe. And it also means stimulative action in Germany, for example, to support a more adequate growth in domestic demand. And they ought to ask whether it makes sense to leave the bulk of the U.S. adjustment on the import side. What would happen to world trade, economic relationships, and prosperity if U.S. imports were suddenly to be cut back is very unpleasant to contemplate. It would be immeasurably better for the health of the global economy for the United States to be able to export its way out of trade deficit, and the time has come for that process to get underway. No sane person would favor the alternative.

I for one applaud the turnaround in attitudes and approach by Secretary Baker and his new team in Washington. I firmly believe that it deserves the kind of support from Europe that has already been forthcoming from Japan. Now is the time to begin restoring a better balance in international trade. Otherwise there is a grave risk that those who seek to maintain a basically open international trading system will lose credibility and those U.S. politicians who would otherwise prefer not to embrace protectionism will lose patience. The ultimate cost to us all would be awesome if the United States were forced to close down its markets because of the lack of any reasonable alternative.

The United States as a Net Debtor Country
International Investment Position of the United States
(Billions of dollars)

	U.S. assets abroad	Foreign assets in the U.S.	U.S. international investment position
1975	295.1	220.9	74.2
1976	347.2	263.6	83.6
1977	379.1	306.4	72.7
1978	447.8	371.7	76.1
1979	510.6	416.1	94.5
1980	606.9	500.8	106.0
1981	719.7	579.0	140.7
1982	839.8	692.0	147.0
1983	893.8	787.6	106.2
1984	914.7	886.4	28.2
Jan.–June 1985	917.9	925.9	−8.0

	1980	1981	1982	1983	1984
Direct Investment (year-end)					
U.S. investment abroad	215.4	228.3	221.8	227.0	223.4
Foreign official assets in the U.S.	83.0	108.7	124.7	137.1	159.6
Official Assets (year-end)					
U.S. official reserves assets	26.8	30.1	34.0	33.7	34.9
Foreign official assets in the U.S.	176.1	180.4	189.2	194.5	199.0
Private Financial Assets (year-end)					
U.S. private financial assets abroad	301.2	392.8	508.8	553.9	561.7
Foreign private financial assets in the U.S.	241.7	289.8	378.1	456.0	527.9
Foreign Lending by U.S. Banks					
Net new lending	46.8	84.2	111.1	29.9	8.5
Loans outstanding (year-end)	203.9	293.5	404.6	434.5	443.0

The U.S. Current Account
(Billions of Dollars)

	1983	1984	1985 (first half)
Net trade	−62.0	−108.3	−62.5
Net services	30.1	18.2	6.9
Government transfers	−9.0	−11.6	−6.5
Current account deficit	−40.8	−101.5	−62.1

The U.S. Dollar and Foreign Exchange Rates

A. *Weighted Average Value of the Dollar: 1980–1982 = 100*

$1980 = 90.7$
$1981 = 99.5$
$1982 = 109.8$

	1983	1984	1985
Jan.	109.7	119.1	132.0
Feb.	111.0	117.3	136.0
Mar.	112.0	115.3	136.9
Apr.	112.5	116.7	131.7
May	112.2	119.4	131.9
Jun.	114.3	120.2	130.4
Jul.	115.1	124.1	125.8
Aug.	116.9	124.0	124.0
Sep.	116.7	127.3	125.3
Oct.	114.8	128.5	118.9
Nov.	116.4	126.8	117.0
Dec.	118.0	129.4	116.1

The U.S. Dollar and Foreign Exchange Rates—*Continued*

B. Foreign Exchange Rates
   (in units of foreign currency per U.S. dollar)

	1979		1980		1981	
	D Mark	Yen	D Mark	Yen	D Mark	Yen
Jan.	1.850	197.75	1.724	237.87	2.009	202.35
Feb.	1.875	200.48	1.748	244.32	2.139	205.68
Mar.	1.860	206.31	1.850	248.45	2.105	208.77
Apr.	1.896	216.26	1.876	250.13	2.164	214.96
May	1.908	218.34	1.791	228.47	2.294	220.65
Jun.	1.884	218.58	1.767	217.91	2.378	224.11
Jul.	1.824	216.50	1.747	221.09	2.440	232.29
Aug.	1.829	217.91	1.790	223.86	2.501	233.21
Sep.	1.793	222.42	1.790	214.41	2.350	229.46
Oct.	1.790	230.36	1.842	209.29	2.254	231.48
Nov.	1.771	244.92	1.919	213.08	2.229	223.02
Dec.	1.734	240.33	1.970	209.42	2.258	218.96

	1982		1983		1984	
	D Mark	Yen	D Mark	Yen	D Mark	Yen
Jan.	2.294	224.82	2.389	232.72	2.811	233.81
Feb.	2.366	235.29	2.428	236.13	2.698	233.59
Mar.	2.380	241.25	2.411	238.27	2.597	225.28
Apr.	2.397	244.08	2.440	237.76	2.648	225.23
May	2.313	236.97	2.467	234.74	2.749	230.47
Jun.	2.429	251.19	2.549	240.04	2.740	233.59
Jul.	2.466	255.04	2.591	240.50	2.849	243.07
Aug.	2.481	259.07	2.674	244.44	2.886	242.25
Sep.	2.506	263.30	2.668	242.37	3.031	245.46
Oct.	2.532	271.59	2.603	232.88	3.067	246.73
Nov.	2.554	264.06	2.685	235.02	2.999	243.55
Dec.	2.420	241.95	2.750	234.47	3.103	247.83

	1985	
	D Mark	Yen
Jan.	3.171	254.19
Feb.	3.289	260.42
Mar.	3.298	257.93
Apr.	3.095	251.83
May	3.105	251.64
Jun.	3.062	244.44
Jul.	2.908	241.14
Aug.	2.793	237.36
Sep.	2.838	236.57

The U.S. Current Account Deficit and Total World Savings: 1982-1984 (Billions of Dollars)

		1982	1983	1984
1)	U.S. current account deficit	11	41	102
2)	ROECD financial savings[a]	360	360	360
3)	RoW financial savings[b]	470	470	470
4)	Line 1 as a percentage of line 3	2	9	22

a. Financial balance of household sector at current prices converted into dollars at current exchange rates.
b. ROECD savings increased by a factor of 1.3 to account for the financial savings in non-OECD countries.
Note: ROECD (OECD countries excluding the United States)
      RoW (World excluding the United States)

Ratio of Savings to Disposable Personal Income (Percent)

Period	U.S.	France	F.R. Germany	Italy	U.K.	Japan	Canada
1970	8.0	16.7	14.6	[e]21.6	9.3	18.2	5.3
1979	5.9	16.2	13.9	25.3	14.1	18.7	11.3
1980	6.0	14.9	14.2	22.0	15.2	19.2	12.3
1981	6.7	15.8	14.9	24.0	13.5	19.7	14.2
1982	6.2	15.7	14.2	24.0	12.9	[r]17.6	15.2
1983	5.0	14.9	12.7	N.A.	10.9	17.3	13.3
1984	6.1	N.A.	N.A.	N.A.	N.A.	N.A.	N.A.

Note: Data are seasonally adjusted except for Japan.

General and Federal Government Deficits and Net Private Savings

(A): *Net Private Savings*
(B): *General government Deficit*
(C): *Federal Government Deficit*

Billions of Dollars
Seasonally adjusted at annual rates

	1983	1984	1984				1985	
			I	II	III	IV	I	II
(A)	194.6	271.6	259.6	260.1	282.5	283.9	241.0	268.6
(B)	−134.5	−122.9	−107.4	−109.2	−133.0	−142.2	−111.4	−163.8
(C)	−178.6	−175.8	−161.3	−163.7	−180.6	−197.8	−165.1	−214.1
(B:A)	−.69	−.45	−.41	−.42	−.47	−.50	−.46	−.61
(C:A)	−.92	−.65	−.62	−.63	−.64	−.70	−.69	−.80

Financing the U.S. Trade Deficit
  (Billions of Dollars)

	1983	*1984*	*1985* *(first half)*
Current Account	− 40.8	− 101.5	− 62.1
Financed by:			
Net bank flow	19.4	23.2	12.7
Net other private capital	3.7	40.9	16.4
Net direct investment	6.6	18.0	4.7
Errors and omissions	11.5	24.7	25.9
Foreign official flows	− 0.4	− 5.2	− 3.1